7th Circle

For David
who captured the
essence of Fray Marc,
Maggie—

by Maggie Jaffe

Books by the author

7th Circle

Continuous Performance

How The West Was One

1492: What Is It Like To Be ***Discovered?***
(with Deborah Small)

The Body Politic

The Prisons

ISBN: 1-891812-07-6
Second Edition

Grateful acknowledgment is made to the following magazines and anthologies where some of these poems first appeared: *And What Rough Beast: Poems At The End Of The Century; Bakunin; Bullhead; Cedar Hill Review; Chiron Review; Conspire; European Judaism; Famous Women; House Organ; Kafka; Minnesota Review; Pemmican; Pieces of Eight: A Women's Anthology of Verse; Pif Magazine; Rattle; Semi-Dwarf Review; Viet Nam Generation; Vol. No; War, Literature & The Arts; The Women's Review of Books.*

For their editorial comments, I wish to thank Robert Edwards, Roger Taus, Karla Donahue, LaRae Cunningham, Carol Kushner, Kerstin Stuerzbecher, and Deborah Small. With special thanks to Christopher Presfield for his invaluable support. Honorable mention to Tosh the cat.

Cover: *7th Circle: Woods Of The Suicides*, Deborah Small.

An asterisk (*) in the text refers to the "Notes" page.

Cedar Hill Publications
Senior Editor: ***Christopher Presfield***
Managing Editor: ***Gloria Doyle***
3722 Hwy. 8 West
Mena, AR 71953
(501) 394-7029

for Them

Contents

7th Circle 7

Comrades, Mayakovsky 8

Marina Tsvetayeva 10

Last Days of Georg Trakl 11

Saint Jean 12

Paul Celan 15

For Lewis B. Puller, Jr. 16

Photos By Diane Arbus 18

Van Gogh's Whore 20

Maria Callas 21

World Of Dust 22

Everything Happens At Night 24

Walter Benjamin 27

Kafka At Work 28

A Brief History of 20th Century Art 31

Otto Dix: Artist Against War 32

I: Great Good War 33

II: Trench Warfare, 1915-18 35

III: *Self-Portrait as Mars* 36

IV: Demobbed, Berlin, 1923 38

V: Degenerate Art, 1937 40

VI: Prisoner of War, 1945 42

Notes & List of Illustrations 44

The Word as Wound 46

Afterword by Joe Napora

7th Circle

Under Massachusetts law, a suicide is to be denied a Christian burial; that his body be buried near a highway or a crossroads; and that "a Cart-load of Stones" be laid upon his grave "as a Brand of Infamy, and a warning to others to beware of the like Damnable practices."

—H. Kushner, *Self-Destruction in the Promised Land*

Comrades, Mayakovsky

January, 1930:
in his hog heaven
Stalin's a Jew
interrogated by the KGB
for writing lyrical poems
that don't raise class consciousness.
The Revolution's led by workers
who love to fuck—not the usual
motherfuckers—& vodka
flows like the Don.
No one is starved for love.

April, 1930:
in his nightmare he's
naked at the podium
while students mock
his dada. He shouts back,
but his voice is shot.
He's a marigold in winter
who thought his poetry's built
to last, like the Bridge he saw
in Whitman's "dollar-
grubbing" America.

Comrades,
    Mayakovsky
clutched a rivet
only the rivet metamorphosed
into a gun
pointing straight at his heart:
        Art.

Marina Tsvetayeva

As a child of three she had
"a frenzied wish to become lost."
Later, exiled in Paris or in *Praha,*
hunger artists walk contorted streets,
chain smoke cigarettes so that
poems may breathe.
A passport photo shows dark-
eyed, angular-faced Marina
who finally got what she asked for.
Rilke, Pasternak & the two
Sophias were a few of her lovers.
Back in the USSR, they won't even
hire her as a dishwasher.

To Stalin, she was a fascist for interrogating
the Revolution; to Fascists, a Red dupe
for defending Mayakovsky's art.
Who in Russia didn't know the poetry of
Marina Ivanova Tsvetayeva?

After hanging herself
from a "crude black hook,"
she was laid in an unmarked grave
not even her daughter could find.
August, 1941: *This is how they sharpen knives on stones.* *

Last Days Of Georg Trakl

Three things he loved:
cigarettes dipped in opium,
the black pool of his exquisite poetry
& his own sister, stoned
on laudanum.

Dissolute days in the *Gymnasium,*
drugged nights without money,
enlists in the Austrian army.

As a pharmacist, sent to the
Eastern Front. Runs out of morphine.
Charged with 90 wounded
men carried into a barn.
Above the shattered limbs of soldiers,
the moon explodes.
White hands gnaw walls,
"wild lament of their broken mouths." *

Help me, help them! No response.
Until one soldier blows
out his brains with his bolt-action Mauser.
Trakl's nerves are also shot.
Rescued from suicide by his "superiors,"
in the ward, that night, he imbibes
a lethal dose of coke.

Saint Jean

Show her the instruments . . .

Tell us about Jean Seberg.
I hail from Marshalltown, Iowa.
When I was 17, I was chosen
over 18 thousand other girls
to star as the androgynous French
soldier in Otto Preminger's *Saint Joan.*
I also wrote and produced my first play,
Be Kind to Animals, in the 4th grade.

What was Preminger like?
Sadistic, a genius.
I think he was pleased that
my armor caught fire. In this way
I'd learn, like Joan, how to suffer.
My arms and stomach are still scarred.

After *Joan,* you starred in Preminger's
Bonjour Tristesse,* Godard's *Breathless,
***Lilith, Paint Your Wagon* and**
Romain Gary's *Birds of Peru.*
How is it to work with a husband-director?
Romain thinks all women are whores
and all men sons of whores.
I detested the roles he created for me.

Friends say you're insecure
about your appearance. Yet you're
blessed with that ideal, American look.
In America, blonde hair and blue-gray eyes
are always equated with beauty—and
beautiful women should keep
their legs spread, mouths shut.

Politics?
I joined the NAACP at 14.
I also supported the Black Panthers,
which is why the FBI keeps harassing me
by disseminating lies that
Jamal Hakim is the father of my child.
But Hoover himself is a queen and a mulatto.

The war?
While one man lands on the moon,
thousands die in mud in Vietnam.

And men?
My first marriage was to Francois Moreuil.
Divorced him to marry Romain Gary,
whom I left for Clint Eastwood.
After Clint, Jamal. I was Jamal's honky;
he was unstable.

Carlos Fuentes was my Mexican lover.
I use rose-scented spray on my pussy
because my body is also revolutionary.
I like men but don't really trust them.

How would you sum up the *real* Jean Seberg?

I run too fast
I fly too high
I hit too hard
Too wide my eyes
Too full my heart
*Too deep the pain.**

Paul Celan

You didn't die
the mauve death . . .

Here is a man.
Here is a despised man,
a pariah with a human tongue.
In his mother tongue
speaks good German:
*"der Tod ist ein Meister aus Deutschland."**
Here is a rifle and a bullet.
Here his mother, her ash-
colored hair streaked with blood.
Here is an oven, here a shovel.
Here a man digs his own grave
while another man drinks,
he drinks ice-clear vodka,
his eyes are blue.
Here is a man moved to stone.
No stone to mark his mother's
grave: bone, ash, smoke.
Here is a stranger without papers,
a rucksack filled with poems.
Black sun, mute earth,
River Seine is home.

For Lewis B. Puller, Jr.

Our stumps are all tangled up.

Chesty pulled more than his weight.
The Marine Corps had to love him,
couldn't pin enough medals
on his chest for fighting 5
wars & for having a son.
Dad taught me to stand for ladies
& to shake a man's hand firmly.

But life rushes right by a man.
In a *flash*—Virginia childhood, to San Diego,
to the triple-canopied jungle—steps on a
booby-trapped howitzer round,
vaporized legs, pink mist surrounds him.
Pray, Lieutenant, for God's sake, pray.
Screams seem to come from another country.
Years later, Pain still walks point for him.

Back in the World
a wife & kids, booze & pain-killers.
Demands clemency for vets who've deserted,
then loses a bid for Congress.
A '91 photo shows clench-jawed
Puller in front of the Wall:
his wheelchair mirrored
in the smooth granite surface.

May 11, 1994: Lewis B. Puller, Jr.
died of a *self-inflicted wound*
19 years after the war's end,
the average age of a grunt in Vietnam.

Photos By Diane Arbus

Few people have the imagination for reality.

If you photographed the real
Diane Arbus, who would we see?
A cranky, crying girl,
always hot & tired.

Which childhood memories obsess you?
Bubba forcing me to eat
until I'm so fat, nobody loves me.

What would your marriage photos divulge?
Allan walking out on me
for a Hollywood actress.
Two terrific kids who scare me.
Both of us making it in high-gloss magazines.

When you're shooting people,
with whom do you feel an affinity?
Normal looking crazy people,
dwarves & giants, bag ladies,
insomniacs, alkies & junkies.

If you personified?
death, who would s/he be?

Me in the bathtub,
wrists slit, white spit
on blue lips, pink water
& gray tile. The faucet drips.

Van Gogh's Whore

He was strange.
He'd rage so quiet
in his corner,
no sound but pipe *chomp*,
mouse-scratching pen
to paper—all the while he'd go
on about the poor.

At first I nearly fainted:
a gray-white shriveled
mushroom.
But I said to myself,
get hold of yourself.
You've dropped two,
buried one,
you even lived through war!
deep red
gone to black. To bone.
A stiff prick's better,
my bread and butter.

If I hold his ear up to mine,
it's not the sea I'd hear
but his—our own—mute howling.

Maria Callas

Dark eyed, bird-like,
she made herself
svelte.
Her crystal voice
needed constant honing.
Audiences loved how
she suffered for Art.
She loved a billionaire
who instead married Jackie K.
For publicity? for kinky sex?
In Pasolini's *Medea,*
her last performance,
she wouldn't sing
but she's riveting
as the beautiful, tragic
infanticide.
Pharmaceuticals and
booze destroyed her voice.
She died in Paris alone.
Well, her maid was with her.

World Of Dust

My grandfather trudged
2000 *versts* through pine dark
forests, calf deep snow to America,
then out of his life.
He was cruel.
His carpenter's tools
collected dust
in the room's dark corner.

By fifty, grandmother's
face was geography:
lines of demarcation,
a dried-up river bed.
Her hands, like gnarled oaks,
plucked chickens in the New
World where dog eats dog
eats . . .
Essen, meine Kinder,
black bread, whitefish,
cabbage stew.

My father walked the Thirties
carrying bales of cloth,
saw a suicide once
at Chambers and Wall.

Invested [World War II] in rubber,
in '45 he marries my mother.
Myself: 1948.

I step out of my car
emptied of singing
to work, to work.
Emptied by news of war,
the hungry, radiation
seepage into veins of the earth.

Mostly I am sick of fathers.
My father's implacable silence,
my grandfather found hanged
from an Ailanthus [tree of heaven]
in Brooklyn—without testament
to the living.

Everything Happens At Night

(In Memory, Steve Biko, died September 12, 1977)

In South Africa
everything happens at night.
Night held captive, smeared,
retched
in Soweto, Nyanga, Sharpeville . . .
At railway stations, cinemas,
restaurants, toilets
("Non-Whites Only"),
color itself is void.

Copper sun, sere earth,
weaver bird song,
mealie fields at dusk.
In the veldt, night
is lion-tongue,
giraffe-knowing,
antelope-grace
impressed on pale
gold Krugerrands.

Suburban swimming pools,
chained guard dogs, white
walls splashed with bougainvillea,
protea, cape primrose.
In Black townships only thorn
trees survive.

"When I'm nervous," she says,
"I have a double scotch
and clean my husband's rifle."
Outside, the Karoo *dorp*
bellows like a wounded wildebeest.
Waiting for what?

Steve Biko, brain injury.
Jacob Monakgotla, heart attack.
James Lenkoe, natural causes.
Dumisani Mbatha, unknown illness.
Joseph Mdluli, application of force to neck.
Lawrence Ndzanga, natural causes.
Neil Aggett, hanged himself.
Sifundile Matalasi, self-strangulation.
Thabo Mosala, internal bleeding.
"Looksmart" S. Ngudle, suicide by hanging.
J.B. Tubakwe, suicide by hanging.
Ahmed Timol, fell out of tenth story window.
Solomon Modipane, suicide by hanging.
Ernest Dipale, hanged himself.

"Official Version,"
yet their names snake
through unrecorded history
like the yellow Molopo River.

In *shebeens* not enough
brandy to wash-
clean their dying
    not enough night—
Business as usual in the mines,
extricating gold and diamond
bullets: "Nigger rhymes with trigger"
in this suck, suck, suck hole
South Africa.

"South African police and Black
rioters battle in the township
of Soweto.
Killed: thirty-two.
Wounded: three hundred."
    Nyana we sizwe: brothers of the land,
    here is where you stand.
    There *is* witness.

Walter Benjamin

dreamt of a labyrinth- like
bookstore and was happy.
Then woke in Vichy, France,
Autumn, 1940.
Frankly, he's unlucky—
more dreamer than schemer,
equating scheming with Capital.
Which is why he's at this sealed-
off border, crossing into the only
country that will have him.
His suicide "so profoundly moved
the guards," they allowed his
comrades passage into Spain,
god damn them.
Were his books with his
"unintelligible marginalia"
beside him?

Unintelligible to whom?

`Self`
`alienation`
`has reached`
`a point that`
`it experiences`
`its own`
`destruction as`
`aesthetic`
`pleasure.`

`Fascism`
`aestheticizes`
`politics which`
`culminates`
`in one thing:`

<u>`War`</u>`.`

Kafka At Work

Kafka At Work

Alef

The Workers' Accident Insurance office
& K is hardly working.
Instead, he doodles this:
gaunt man weighted with sorrow.
Winter, eastern Europe,
coal-yellow smoke, genteel moldering
of the Bohemian Empire.

Bet

K looks in the mirror,
sees his weakness.
Coughs up blood, *hides it*
from other working stiffs.
Daydreams about sex like the rest of us:
Milena, the *shiksa's* pear-shaped ass.

Dalet

After work, studies
The Kabbala and Zola's *J'Accusé!* *
Reads the latest mystery
& news from the Front.
Should he enlist? Not when his
"lungs conspire behind his back."

gimmel

By 9 o'clock, everyone's
stuffed, but not Kafka.
Now his real work begins:
Metamorphosis   hunger   guilt
Terror   *Amerika*   brute father . . .

mem

Kafka dies at 41 years of age in 1924.
Before his death, he instructs Max
to "burn all his work,"
then he consents to publication.
Years later, Milena & his 3 sisters
are incinerated in Auschwitz:
their body's ash mixing
with mountains of bones.
Tak.

shin

Even Hitler, a "devout" vegetarian,
couldn't resist Czech sausage & dumplings
after triumphantly crushing Prague.
Washed it down with rivers of blood:
Kafkaesque.

A Brief History of 20th Century Art

Gestapo officer pointing
to Picasso's *Guernica:*
—Did you do this?
—No, you did.

Otto Dix

Artist Against War

I: Great Good War

1914: After he enlists
in the German army
Dix finalizes his
Self-Portrait as a Soldier.
Boyish features
of his earlier paintings
become *brut*: shaved head,
grossly thickened neck & mouth;
fierce black eyes skewer the civilian viewer.
Awash in red, he
metamorphoses into *War*.

Along with his rifle, flak jacket
& helmet, Dix carries the *Bible,*
Nietzsche's *Joyful Wisdom,*
sketch pad & pen into battle.
Later, as a machine gun guard
on the western front, he'll write:
"War is something bestial: hunger, lice,
mud, rats, gases, canons & insanity."

II: Trench Warfare, 1915-18

Freshly killed corpse "grins" & farts next to him.
Dix swallows food, wipes hands on mud-
caked pants, then sketches the corpse.
If paint could scream, ringing in ears,
up & down the line, within his restless sleep . . .
Dix has the hollowed-eyed vacant
stare of a "grunt."
In reality he's an artist-worker,
the battlefield suggestive of his gaping
wounds or of a vagina.
"Ultimately, all wars are fought
over and for the sake of the vulva."

III: *Self-Portrait As Mars*

1915: angles & planes after Cubism,
Dix draws himself as
    GOD OF WAR.
Encompassing the figure are splotches
of blood, teeth biting into blood,
a runaway horse, white eyes
rolling. Also half-ruined
buildings & burst-open cities.
[Image from recurring dream: he *must* crawl
through blasted houses without issue.]
Prophetic. In the night sky above the carnage
at Battle of the Somme, the red
planet rises to the east.

IV: Demobbed, Berlin, 1923

Stump-legged enlistee.
Face chunked out where he took mortar.
Skeleton works its way through his flesh.
With his one good eye, he looks
up at her ass. She laughs.
Adjusts her shawl.
He smells cordite, sweat,
sweet-sour corpse
in which he landed, face down.
He carries the corpse's stench like a cross.

Jazz throbs from Cabaret *Amerika*
where the cocksuckers dance
or grope each other's flesh.
The cripple hates their smug faces,
especially the bushman drummer.
Let him go back to Africa.

Hunger is a chain-linked barbed-wire
fence he's stuck behind.
Through the fence, the cripple sees
the bloated Jew. Reds & Jews.
Hence he's all ears to young Adolf,
the co[s]mic house painter.

Standing in the shadowed corner, Dix.
Sketches the crippled vet & the whore as
Two Victims of Capitalism.
She: pock-marked by the clap.
He: wasted by mortar.

V: Degenerate Art, 1937

Dix, Beckmann, Chagall, Grosz, Heartfield,
Kandinsky, Klee, El Lissitzky . . .
"degenerate" because they won't paint
golden bodies for the Reich.
In Goebbels' "art" catalogue
Dix's *War Cripples* cited as
"sabotage of the national defense."

In '33, stripped of his post as art teacher.
Turns the corner—there's the Gestapo.
Could he, should he,
get him in a stranglehold?
Black tongue thrust
from the Nazi skull.
Better: he'll sketch him.

Politics bore him,
prefers whorehouses.
They're alive & so [he thinks] is he.
But not the conscript he cradled one night—
guts spilling out all over his hands.

So. Night sweats continue.
His wife snaps on the light,
bombs burst in air.
His screams drowned out by
thudding boots, raucous calls:
Jews Out!

VI: Prisoner of War, 1945

Turns out, Dix's service as a soldier
is far from over.
In '45 when he's 54,
he's drafted into the *Volkssturm,*
a home defense unit.
Separated from his unit
& taken by the French as a POW.
He's recognized. Forced to paint
de Gaulle posters in exchange for food.

Demobbed again, he draws
Self-Portrait as a Prisoner of War:
an old man with a deeply lined face
imprisoned behind barbed wire.
Behind him, two others—
one depicted as The Fool.
Instead of the "dominating"
red of his youth, he now employs
gray, green & blue.

Dix died one year after '68:
banner year for "free love,"
worldwide Revolution,
devastating casualties in the Vietnam War.

Notes & Illustrations

Marina Tsvetayeva: quote from "Poem of the End," 1924.

Last Days Of Georg Trakl: quote from "Grodek," 1914.

Saint Jean: August, 1979: despondent over accidentally aborting her child during a suicide attempt, Jean Seberg climbed into the backseat of her Renault with two month's supply of barbiturates. Her body was not found for ten days. Romain Gary accused the FBI of "destroying" her. He even speculated that she was murdered. He committed suicide soon after.

Paul Celan: A German speaking Romanian Jew, Celan spent two years in a German death camp removing rubble. When he was released, he learned of his parents' death: his mother was shot by the Nazis. He emigrated to Paris in 1948 and committed suicide by drowning in 1970. "Death is a Master from Germany" is from "Death Fugue," a poem which he later distanced himself from for being "too explicit."

Kafka At Work: In 1894, Emile Zola's *J'Accusé!* defended Captain Alfred Dreyfus against charges of treason and also denounced the French military for its anti-Semitism. Dreyfus' trial obsessed Kafka for his adult life.
Tak: Czech for "so."

Otto Dix: Artist Against War (1891-1969)

Self-Portrait with Carnation (1912).

I: *Self-Portrait as a Soldier* (1914).

II: *Shellhole with Flowers* (1916).

III: *Self-Portrait as Mars* (1915).

IV: *Two Victims of Capitalism* (1923).

V: *War Cripples* (1920). Exhibited in the Degenerate Art Show, thereafter destroyed by the Nazis. In total, 16,000 paintings by 1,400 artists were destroyed.

VI: *Self-Portrait as a Prisoner of War* (1947).

The Word as Wound

by Joe Napora

You have seen how difficult it is to decipher
the script with one's eyes, but our man deciphers
it with his wounds.

—Franz Kafka, "In the Penal Colony"

Maggie Jaffe's *7th Circle* is a poetic journey through the seventh circle of Dante's *Inferno,* the domain of the suicides. For Jaffe, though, suicide is more than it appears to be, and these poems show us that the Inferno is more extensive than we would like to believe it to be. Spanning the twentieth century (Van Gogh [1898] to Lewis Puller, Jr. [1994]), Jaffe's poems are also an indictment of the politics of suicide (fascism, Stalinism) and the history that drives people to suicide (the Vietnam War, anti-Semitism).

First is Mayakovsky, the poet of the revolution, who compromised his poetry in service to the State: "in his nightmare he's / naked at the podium/ while students mock / his dada." His dada? Yes, dadaism but also his daddy: early on Joseph Stalin said of Mayakovsky, "Indifference to his memory and for his work is a crime." Jaffe's poem alludes to Whitman's (Brooklyn) Bridge but also to Hart Crane, another suicide, with Mayakovsky's "rivet" turning into a bullet, used against himself. And another allusion develops, to Crane and to Whitman's "Brooklyn Ferry," with the rivet reminding us that Mayakovsky's last poem / suicide note read: "Love's boat has smashed against the daily grind."

In "Comrades, Mayakovsky," the line has it that the rivet "metamorphosed / into a gun," not "changed." Hence the poem also connects us to Kafka, just as "Marina Tsvetayeva" does with its "hunger artists." And the Tsvetayeva poem leads us back, to re-trace the steps of our reading with "Mayakovsky's art" and reference to Stalin, and forward again with its "crude black hook," which is nothing other than the question mark (Why suicide?) that inheres in almost every one of these poems.

"Last Days of Georg Trakl" introduces the theme of the soldier suicide, developed more in "Saint Jean," carried forward with the Puller poem (whose father, Chesty Puller, warred against Nicaragua's Sandino), and brought to culmination in the Otto Dix sequence.

"Saint Jean" is set out as an interrogation, mimicking and mocking the Inquisition's questioning of Joan of Arc: "When I was 17, I was chosen / over 18 thousand other girls / to star as the androgynous French / soldier in Otto Preminger's *Saint Joan.*" And of course it is the Inquisition continued with those other sadistic "fathers": Preminger, J. Edgar Hoover, and husband, Romain Gary. The form itself recalls the later interrogation / interview poem about Diane Arbus, the interview as torture.

"Paul Celan" ends with two compelling images. One is of the impotent poet: "Here is a stranger without papers / a rucksack filled with poems." The irony of the effacement of the poet's identity, because of the non-possession of political papers, is in contrast to the surplus of poetry he carries, the only thing that provides for the poet's true identity, the only thing that might save the poet (and the reader). Everything conspires to keep us from the very papers that lead to something we can call redemption. The final image is allusive but as important. "Black sun, mute earth, / River Seine is home" recalls the words of Tsvetayeva: "So long as you are a poet, you shall not perish in the elemental, for everything brings you back into the element of elements: the word." The Word is our only way out of this world of pain and betrayal, the word our true home.

Remember that reactionary slogan of a few years back, "The personal is political"? Jaffe turns these paralyzing words back onto themselves, making them radical, by showing the political as personal: "my grandfather found hanged / from an Ailanthus [tree of heaven] / in Brooklyn". And Jaffe's "Mostly I am sick of fathers" becomes a sickness of all those sadistic fathers: grandfather, political leaders, generals, the old men sending the young off to die.

The Otto Dix sequence is one of the most compelling anti-war poems I've ever read. Dix demonstrated the essential lie of the fascist aesthetic, that war is glorious. He was persecuted for the truth: war cripples the body as well as the spirit. His lesson is never fully learned. The number of Vietnam vets' suicides, remember, is greater than those who fell in combat. Dix's paintings and Jaffe's poems expose the lie of warfare, and the real attraction of the fascist to the crippled and maimed. Wasted by violence, redemption is only possible through more violence. It's a cripple's logic, but it's pervasive.

> *There were perhaps only two Jews in my class*
> *possessed of courage and both shot themselves*
> *while still at school or shortly after.*
>
> —Franz Kafka, *Diaries, 1914-1923.*

Kafka's writing is always personal and, hence, political. As he lay dying, not only was he making the final preparation for the publication of "The Hunger Artist" but during his last days he was unable to eat. He had reached the end of the struggle that lead finally to annihilation. A suicide? Perhaps not legally, technically, but in fact, yes, by his own logic, as a writer he was a suicide.

The writer, for Kafka (and the age) is a self-exterminator. Jaffe understands this when she brings history back into Kafka's work: Kafka as Jew and anarchist, as writer: "Years later, Milena & his 3 sisters / are incinerated in Auschwitz— / their body's ash mixing /

with mountains of bones." This is essential service to a writer who critics have attempted to remove from history. Jaffe also understands something more crucial to all writers: Kafka never found his way out of the dilemma of Writing through writing. He was well aware of what writing cost him. No writer was so aware! No wonder he asked Max Brod to burn all of his writings when he died.

By its own example as Writing, *7th Circle* attempts the impossible: it provides an alternative to fragmentation, isolation, and the despair leading to suicide. And genuine writing is the only political act left to the hunger artist within the penal colony.

Andi Olsen

Originally from New York, Maggie Jaffe lives in San Diego and teaches at San Diego State University. In 1993-94 she was a visiting lecturer at Masaryk University, the Czech Republic. She is a recipient of a 1997 California Arts Council grant and is Poetry Editor of *Cedar Hill Review* and Editorial Assistant of *Rattle.*

Cedar Hill Publications
3722 Hwy. 8 West
Mena, Arkansas 71953

96 SONNETS FACING CONVICTION—Leonard Cirino
$10.00—Poetry
ISBN: 1-891812-20-3

GRAY AIR—Christopher Presfield
$8.00—Poetry
ISBN: 1-891812-15-7

7th CIRCLE—Maggie Jaffe
$10—Poetry
ISBN: 1-891812-07-6

AMNESIA TANGO—Alan Britt
$10—Poetry
ISBN: 1-891812-14-9

THE BOOK OF ALLEGORY—Michael McIrvin
$10—Poetry
ISBN:1-891812-03-3

"EDEN, OVER . . ."—Tim Scannell
$5—Poetry
ISBN:1-891812-01-7

PIECES OF EIGHT: A Women's Anthology of Verse
$10—Poetry
ISBN:1-891812-02-5

THE TERRIBLE WILDERNESS OF SELF—Leonard Cirino
$10—Poetry
ISBN:1-891812-00-9

THE WORLD AS IT IS—John Taylor
$10—Prose
ISBN: 1-891812-04-1

JAM: Cedar Hill Anthology Series
$10—Poetry
ISBN: 1-891812-05-X

Available from:
Amazon.com
http://www.amazon.com/